Network Marketing Blueprint for Success

Become a Rockstar in Your Network Marketing Business

By Colin K

Disclaimer

The advice contained in this material might not be suitable for everyone. The author obtained the information from sources believed to be reliable and from his own personal experience, but he neither implies nor intends any guarantee of accuracy.

The author, publisher and distributors never give legal, accounting, medical or any other type of professional advice. The reader must always seek those services from competent professionals that can review their own particular circumstances.

The author, publisher and distributors particularly disclaim any liability, loss, or risk taken by individuals who directly or indirectly act on the information contained herein. All readers must accept full responsibility for their use of this material.

All pictures used in this book are for illustrative purposes only. The people in the pictures are not connected with the book, author or publisher and no link or endorsement between any of them and the topic or content is implied, nor should any be assumed. The pictures are only licensed for use in this book and must not be used for any other purpose without prior written permission of the rights holder.

Table of Contents

Chapter 1

Introduction

Network marketing is perhaps the most misunderstood and the most controversial concept of wealth creation. It generates strong emotions. Most of us were invited to a fancy presentation and got excited about the prospect of working from home, firing our boss, no office politics or commuting to work. There was also no cap on the income potential. The prospect of generating great amount passive income excited us as it would give us time to our families, travel the world and pursue our other fantasies. It was better than any retirement plan or job security. It could be started part-time with minimal startup costs.

There were dreams in our eyes of a better future. But then what happened.... Reality broke through. We suffered rejection from our friends and families. Our recruiting drive never took off. We never saw those fancy checks coming into our bank accounts. What happened? Were we lied to by persons who sponsored us or were they also victims of the same lies?

On the other hand, there are people generating great amounts of passive income through their efforts in network marketing. Network marketing is an industry that is experiencing an exponential growth with a turnover of over .... Billion Dollars and over 55 million distributors worldwide. It is being taught as a subject in many business schools around the globe.

People like Warren Buffet and Donald Trump who are not only some of the richest people on the planet but also have the most astute business minds own direct selling companies. Richard Bronson who owns over 300 companies worldwide is involved in network marketing.

Robert Kiyosaki author of 'Rich Dad Poor Dad' book series and one of the greatest financial educators recommends network marketing as the 'Perfect Business' to achieve financial freedom and security. Then we have Robert G Allen, author of international bestsellers ' Multiple Streams of Income' and the 'One Minute Millionaire' not only endorsing network marketing as one of the best and smart ways to create wealth but also being very successful in the business thereby leading with example.

Why are these business leaders staking their names and fames to promote a business model that has generated so much debate and negativity? They believe network marketing is the wave of the future. The big question is if network marketing is such a great concept then why are so many people failing to make headway after joining the business?

What then is the truth? Were you lied to when you joined a network marketing company? Why did you fail? Did you not work hard enough but still failed? Were you not smart enough to do this business? Did you look yourself in the mirror and call yourself "LOSER" when you failed?

On the other hand, why are so many well-known and respected leaders and educators staking their reputation by strongly advocating network marketing? Is Warren Buffet, who has donated 97% of his wealth to charity, investing in network marketing companies that have an interest of hundreds of thousands of distributors at stake, misleading people? These are difficult questions that need in-depth analysis.

We Dared To Dream!

We are what we are because we have the capacity to dream. It all started because we shared the same dreams....

You, like me, wanted to be your own boss and answer to no one. Financial freedom was important to you. Your time was important to you. You wanted to spend precious time with those you love. You wanted to take your friends and family to dinner and spend $400 without batting an eye or take 2 weeks off and fly to some faraway island on a whim. There was also a deep desire within you for self-fulfillment and also of helping others reach theirs. But now.....

You are fed up with network marketing and the rejection you had to face.

You DON'T want to hear anything more about it.

You are sure that you DON'T want another MLM.

Your DREAMS are all but shattered.......

I want to restore your dreams shattered through misinformation and deception. ***Dreams are the most beautiful part of us.*** The power of our success in life lies in the size of our hopes and DREAMS. We must dare to dream, or we will be lost as human beings.

This is probably the single most important information product I have ever created because of the power of the information it contains. The information contained here will help you to rebuild your dreams. I am here to tell you that it is not your fault. You can regain your dreams with the information in this ebook.

Assuming you follow the instructions in this book as described and with an open mind which is ready to learn, this may be the most important thing you ever read because it will allow you to generate a substantial income. I am talking about the kind of income which will allow you, finally and mercifully, to give up your day job.

My recommendation is that you have a few hours by yourself... away from family and friends. Turn your mobile phone off. Get yourself a cup of your favorite hot drink, close the door and relax. Relax and fully absorb this information because it will change your life for the better.

The information you will gain here will help you easily overcome the obstacles which have prevented you from achieving the success you so desperately want very quickly, improving your financial health significantly. My advice is, therefore, that you take this information very seriously indeed.

Contrary to popular belief, it is possible to make money with network marketing. This book will go some way to dispelling a lot of the untruths and myths surrounding network marketing so that you can get to the crux of what it really takes to of it and I warn you, not all of it will make for comfortable reading. Not knowing the truth is likely to get you into serious financial trouble. This fact will become increasingly apparent as you read this book.

For me, there are two ways of earning an income. Active income is where you work and earn money for each hour that you work. When you are in a job you are paid on an hourly basis. This is active income.

The second way of earning is residual income, where you work once and get paid again and again for the rest of your life.

Unfortunately, society is structured so that the majority of people, and I am talking 99 percent here, are engaged in chasing this active income. I was sick a few years ago and could not work. As a result, my income dried up. My wife and children had to support me. I then made a conscious decision to focus on earning residual income.

I have applied this philosophy to my growing property portfolio, my published books and to my network marketing businesses. This approach has generated a multi-million dollar income for me in a relatively short period of time. Having been in a financial rut myself, I have dedicated my life to teaching others the many things that I have learned along the way.

I have learned that network marketing is by far the quickest and easiest way of generating substantial cash flow. It is cash flow, which enables you, to live the life of your dreams without being tied down to something because your cash is tied up in some business or other. Cash flow allows you to invest in things like property over time and become rich.

Building a property portfolio does create wealth in the long term. You have to wait while you build up equity. Equity is not the same thing as cash flow. Some may argue that equity can be converted into cash. This logic is flawed because if you turn equity into cash you increase debt. It is difficult to rely on a property portfolio for cash flow until such time you can pay a large portion of your mortgage.

The best source for cash flow is business. If you are new to the game then start with network marketing. It is a business you can start with least amount of capital and risk.

I have had traditional businesses and mortgages. The times when I struggled to pay my bills and salaries of my employees were some of the unhappy times in my life.

I tried network marketing and failed because I did not understand the truth behind it, but when I learned the truth and started to generate huge amounts of cash flow, my life changed significantly for the better. Now, all of my mortgages and bills are paid, and I have a significant cash flow to do the things that I want to do with my life, I have never been happier.

This is not because money bought me happiness. We all know that money cannot buy you happiness, but what it bought me is financial freedom. The freedom to do the things I want to do when I want to do them. All because of knowing the truth about network marketing.

Let me tell you, I am not a special case. I am just an ordinary guy who learned the truth and made big money. There are many others just like me who have also made it. If I and so many other ordinary folks can do it, ANYONE can do it, and that includes YOU. In the next chapter, we will go on to dispel some of the false truths and myths about network marketing so that you do not make the same mistakes that I made.

Chapter 2

The Truth about Network Marketing

What I am about to say in this section may cause offense to some people. However, it is important for me to tell the truth about network marketing. I do not believe in sugar coating anything because not telling the truth means that you could end up losing tons of money. I am here to help you to make money in network marketing. You must take the information seriously if you are serious about making money. Not to do so could cause you to go broke. You have been warned...

Because you are reading this book, you will benefit from the two years I spent gathering this information and learning through experience and pain, the real truth about successful network marketing. The truth is that corporate downsizing means that, in this day and age, there is no such thing as job security. The truth is that if you do not accept the truth about network marketing, you may as well go get cozy with your boss in your office and pray that you are not left in the unemployment line with the way that the economy is going. Let us look at a few of these "truths."

TRUTH #1: It Is a Mentoring and Teaching Business

The prevailing belief, unsurprisingly so, is that network marketing is simply about direct sales. Selling products to people.

No..... The truth is, SUCCESSFUL network marketing is about teaching and mentoring people toward THEIR success. NOT your SUCCESS, THEIRS!

The bottom line is that you need to find a good business with a good product. Once you have those under your belt, and you know and understand the business, it is all about mentoring and coaching your team members.

Hearing of THEIR success should be like music to your ears! Help them to achieve their dreams and your success is inevitable. Do you know what active listening is? It is the ability to listen empathetically. To really engage with a person and understand where they are coming from by repeating, paraphrasing and gaining clarity on what they are saying. Network marketing is about listening and understanding in this way, so that you can help people to achieve their lifetime dreams and ambitions.

The secret to my success is mentoring! Coaching other people to success adds meaning and substance to my life. Aside from the fact that I am genuinely helping people to achieve their goals and ambitions, in helping them, ultimately, I help myself.

By ensuring the success of others, my success takes care of itself. Network marketing is probably the only truly spiritual business in the world because of this fact. In network marketing, you do not have to compete with others in order to succeed. The business world is a dog-eat-dog world and competition are what drives it. In network marketing, this need to outsmart the other is neutralized by the fact that you succeed by helping the other, by helping your teammates, they succeed and so do you.

There are a few other home truths to ponder. People who insist on doing everything themselves rarely become wealthy. Those who have the patience to coach others are more likely to become wealthy.

Why is it that some people become wealthy doing network marketing while others do not? The answer is really quite simple. Successful people in any field, really take the time to figure out what makes other people tick. They take the time to work out what motivates other people to do things and why people make the choices that they ultimately make.

Before you go on, you must understand some things about yourself. Before you can mentor others, you must mentor yourself. YOU must take the time to sit down and figure out what exactly motivates YOU to be in this business? Why are you interested in network marketing? It is only by understanding your own motivations that you can truly understand, appreciate and empathize with the motivations of others. Once you are in this state, you can truly mentor others.

Take some time and sit down with a pen and paper. Write down the first thing that comes to your head when you ask yourself WHY. Sit and contemplate it and write down another two reasons. Contemplate those and expand them further until you really get to the heart of the matter and truly understand your own motivations for entering this business.

If you cannot take the time out to do this, you might as well quit now. I may sound harsh, but I can tell you with complete certainty that if you do not understand your own motivations, if you do not know your very personal reasoning behind doing network marketing, you will quit at the very first hurdle that comes along and trust me, there will be many.

Your reason 'why' is what will keep you going when times are tough. You will refer to it over and over again. It is not about money, your 'why' will be something about who you are fundamentally, as a person... When you know and understand your own why, it will make it much easier for you to understand the why of the next person you are trying to convince to join you in your business, as one of your team members.

If you understand and empathize with their why, you will be much more likely to be able to sell to them than any of the hundreds of other home businesses trying to get them on board.

Going back to the money, you may be screaming at the book that yes it is about money, and how the hell does he know that it isn't? Look, when you really break down the motivation for doing anything with regard to making money, money is not really the WHY, it is not the driving factor.

The driving factor is always something bigger than money. Money is simply the tool which is used to get to the WHY. Let me give you some examples, these will help you to pinpoint your own why. Try and add to the list yourself.

<> You want to live in a bigger, more comfortable house.

<> You want to drive a sports car.

<> You want to spend more time with your spouse.

<> You want to spend more time with your kids.

<> You want to learn a new hobby or craft.

<> You want to travel more.

<> You want to help others to change their lives.

<> You want more adventure.

<> What would you most like to give to those whom you love the most?

<> What things make you get emotional?

<> What things make you tick?

Learning to mentor is first about discovering the dreams of those you are mentoring. Discover what motivates a person to get up and do something and you are really onto a serious winner. Discover what people dream about and you can help them create hope and goals. Goals cause people to become more focused in life and focus helps to push people into action.

Dreams create hope. Goals create focus. And focus creates fuel that propels us to action.

You teach people in this business to rediscover their dreams. The difference between their perceived past failures and their future success is this moment. Teach them to work toward their desired future without fears and doubts and there is no limit to their earning potential. They must never compromise on the lifestyle that they wish to create for themselves and their family. It is their birthright to live an abundant life. It is the power of your mentoring that will help you succeed in this business.

TRUTH #2: Network is a "Relationship-Driven" Business

People join people. They don't join companies. They don't care about who the president of the company is or how well the company is being run. You will be surprised to learn that initially, they don't even care about the product. The only thing they care about is you because they can relate to you. They can trust you. No matter how good the products or services, no matter how well-managed the company, you will struggle and go broke if you do not know how to build relationships.

You build relationships when you genuinely care about people. Relationships are developed when you help others to grow physically, mentally, spiritually and financially. You may forget big names in history and politics, you always remember the names of your teachers who helped you through school, friends who gave a helping hand when your chips were down or people who made you feel appreciated and special.

You have to have empathy, and you have to be yourself. You will fail if you try to be someone else other than yourself. The three things that destroy relationships are when you try and gain control over others, be self-righteous and judgmental. Help others with all you have got and the universe will conspire to help you succeed. Practice abundance. It is the essence of relationships. Learn to listen and you will learn more about yourself and foster lifelong relationships.

There is only ONE way to build your network that will last you a lifetime...... It is to build relationships. To achieve that, **you need to become a mentor with a servant's heart**. When you do, people will ask you to, PLEASE sponsor them into your business. If you build your relationships right then, your network will last forever. If you treat your business like just another income source or like a salesperson then you will be trading long-term stability for short-term profit. Your network will collapse.

Direct marketers sell products to the consumer directly. Direct marketers measure their productivity in numbers. Their philosophy is "buy or get out of the way". To Direct Marketers, "relationship-marketing" has a bottom-line VALUE. If they can help they will like to automate relationship-building. Looks 100% real, but it's plastic. If you think like a direct marketer you will fail in this business. If you build relationships and become a mentor with a servant's heart you will succeed.

It is simple. *If you and I work together, we will create an effect much greater than the sum of the parts*. Network marketing (MLM) is not a numbers game, it is a relationship game. Relationship building is the process. It is network marketing.

TRUTH #3: Network Marketing is a Recommendation Business and Not a Sales Business

Network marketing means sharing and transference of your enthusiasm for a product or service. It is a business that works on the recommendation of a product that you use and are excited about. When you see a good movie and have enjoyed watching it, you speak about it to all your friends. You transfer your enthusiasm to your friends. They go and watch the movie because of their trust in your judgment.

If they enjoy the movie, then they will further spread the word to other friends and the viewership of the movie grows. Unfortunately, you don't get paid for spreading the word. Network marketing works in a similar fashion. The only difference is that you get paid for spreading the word.

The fact is you have done word-of-mouth advertising, everyday, since you were a child. You told your mom & dad what you loved and wanted, your favorite ice cream, jeans, baseball bat, books, movies, restaurants, all kinds of things. You've been promoting products since about age 5. But you've never got paid for it. The only difference is that, with network marketing, you get paid every time you recommend someone the product that you love to use. The best part of this business is that you will get checks from this business 25 years from now for a product you recommend to someone today! Isn't that incredible?

More enthusiastic you are about your product or service and more you share it with others joyously, the greater will be the size of your PAYCHECK.

TRUTH #4: You Must Have Belief in the Product to Transfer Your Enthusiasm

In order to transfer your enthusiasm, you must have a BELIEF in the product or service. If you do not have a belief in your product it will show in your body language, in your eyes and behavior pattern. Your heart and mind have to flow in one direction if you are to succeed in this business. If you are artificial you will be found out.

The business will not work for you if your head and heart pull in different directions. If you wish to sponsor someone into the business, then you must believe that network marketing works. Believe that it is one of the best business models to make large amounts of passive income within a remarkably short period of time without financial risks associated with traditional businesses.

How does one build the belief system to succeed? The most important thing is to find a great company, with a strong management and a unique product. Can you recommend ten movies to a friend? Your friend will be confused and will not watch a single movie recommended by you.

You must believe that the product you are promoting is genuinely beneficial to people who use it. To build the belief, you must use the product and find out the benefit for yourself. This is not a selling business. This is a recommendation business based on faith people have in you. You cannot fake this faith by not using the product yourself and try selling it to others.

There are people who believe that the product is just a vehicle to build their network marketing business. Any product will do as long as it brings in money. Such thinking will result in selling a product rather than building a network marketing business that is built on good faith and belief.

Another important thing about belief is that initially when you join a network marketing company your belief system is weak. You have not used the products sufficiently. You know very little about the company you are promoting, and you do not fully understand the business model. Most importantly, you are not making any money so you don't have the confidence. Initially, you have to make considerable effort to learn everything about the business, products, and company. In other words, to build your belief system you have to train yourself extremely hard.

The easiest way to build your belief system is to find a mentor. This is someone who has achieved success in the business. You must be mentored to become a mentor. What you need is to be a part of a mastermind group who wants YOU to succeed. You want up-line leadership support available when you need it.

There is a saying that if you want to make million dollars then mastermind with millionaires. If you want to make $100,000 a year, then be in the company of people who make $100,000 a year. For most people, their yearly income is the average of their 5 people with whom they spend their time. If your 5 closest friends do not have the desired income or goals you aspire for then do not EVER listen to their opinions on business!

If you want to succeed then change your circle of influence. Mastermind with people who are rich and successful and your life will change. This does not mean that you have to dump your friends, just change your circle of influence. Spend more time with your mentor and mastermind group.

Let us say you want to invest in real estate. Would you ask the person who rents one home or a person who owns 25 homes, 14 townhouses, 2 farms and 8 commercial properties? To build a real estate investment business, why would you listen to people who had never invested in their lives? You have to find the right people from whom you can take advice.

In order to build your belief system, you have to be in the company of those who believe in themselves and have succeeded in the business. If you cannot meet your mentor in flesh and blood then watch videos and listen to tapes of people who have achieved impressive results from the business and whom you admire.

Your business will grow in the same proportion as the strength of your belief system. If you are not finding success in your network marketing business then, please check your belief system first. Are you convinced about the product you are using? Are you convinced about the company you are promoting? Are you receiving the right kind of training and support? Are you working with the right kind of mastermind group?

If your belief system is not strong then build your belief system in the product, the compensation plan and the company you are promoting. In case you are not happy then find something you can believe in with your heart and soul. Without strong belief in what you are doing, you are doomed to fail at the very start. If you wish to succeed, then build your belief system first. Let your mind and heart speak as one unit.

Once you have belief in your business then sponsoring will be a fun-filled experience. Your belief will take you from being an exceedingly shy, who is afraid of speaking to strangers, to a market leader who is ready to "share" his product, service and business opportunity with confidence!

Once you have the BELIEF, you will never be defensive about your company or business opportunity. You will create a positive and an emotionally surcharged atmosphere where people will want to be members of your team. You will attract people like a magnet to your business. This electrifying atmosphere is only possible once you learn to speak from your heart that is backed by a strong belief system.

The emotional impact that you produce arises from your inner relationship with your product and program. It does not come from some kind of formula. Emotional power is - thoughtlessness. It bypasses your thinking process, for it has become you. It is your belief system and not something you consciously do or think about, at the moment.

People who succeed in this business is due to their deep belief in the product, the business plan, the company and the people behind the company. They cannot reach the height of success if their hearts and mind did not speak the same language. People converted to their cause because they are emotionally and intellectually honest.

The power of emotional commitment comes from an inner conviction and prospects sense the sincerity even before they speak of committing them to their cause. Once you are convinced regarding the integrity and uniqueness of your product, you will love to share it with others. You can't pretend that something is good when it isn't. When you share your beliefs, you will succeed. Your emotional integrity plays a vital part in your power of personal persuasion. When you have that quality, your prospects will listen with more than just their ears. Your emotions will bypass the prospect's defenses and get to his heart.

Jacob Boehme said it well about 350 years ago. His words still ring true today.

"For realness, the exterior of our life needs to be the signature of the interior."

Your internal belief system will be strong when you sincerely believe that it's right to help people become financially secure. It's right to help people discover a way to better health, personal growth and increased happiness. No wonder, the right kind of network marketing companies can build up loyalty and emotional attachment as few other businesses can! If you don't feel that kind of inner power, then you need to ask yourself if the product line you're marketing is helping you build that emotional power and belief within you.

You cannot sell anything effectively unless you are sold on it yourself. Once you're sold on the products, believe me; you will never have to sell to anyone. The key is to become a user of a great product. Once you start using the product that shows results, you will start sharing the benefits of your experience.

These benefits will fire your inner emotional power. You will then communicate facts. You will share values through emotions. If your listener concludes that your product has great value, it will be because you've shared your emotions and supported them with essential facts. That's a powerful combination, one that lies at the source of the marketing power that you wish to acquire. You can have it. You will have it.

It is important that your emotional power be the servant of intelligence. The closer you are to the unity of truth, the more power you will generate. It is only when knowledge and emotions combine and when heart and mind are one, then great success is achieved. Once you develop the belief system, you won't need any artificial means to find prospects. You will attract prospective associates to you with your warmth, conviction and natural enthusiasm, all of which flow from the center of your being. None of this has to be artificially produced. That is fun!

To achieve this type of belief system, you must have a product or services you really believe in, a compensation plan that generously rewards you and an upline and company leadership that is dedicated to your success. If you have these, then you will have SUCCESS THROUGH *POSITIVE EMOTIONAL POWER.*

TRUTH #5: People Fail Because They Do Not Apply Leverage in Their Network Marketing Business Correctly

Every network marketing company boasts of a compensation plan that creates passive income through leverage. Yet, majority of people who join the business fail because they do not understand how leveraging works.

Most people fail because their focus is on Recruit, Recruit, Recruit, Numbers, Numbers, Numbers! It is a race against time and others to recruit before someone else does. Now you have hundreds of recruits who don't know where they are going. You don't have time to either build relationships or train so many of them. They are left helpless on their own. They start dropping out in hoards. You are back again Recruit, Recruit, Recruit......... This is certainly not leveraging your time or effort.

There are marketers who can recruit dozens, even hundreds, of people through the motivation of greed. When it comes to something sensible and worthwhile, they shy away from becoming involved. This is because they think network market is just a numbers game. They tell their new recruits that they will have spillovers in their downline. That there is no work involved. Lies, Lies, Lies and more Lies........With this kind of thinking, they will attract recruiters who think the same way. No wonder, a culture of 'no work' sets into the organization and the network collapses. They are now back to Recruit, Recruit, Recruit through more greed and lies.

If you have to leverage then, you have to Sponsor, Sponsor, Sponsor....... and .... Retain, Retain, Retain........ There is a BIG difference between a recruiter and a person who sponsors. A recruiter is interested only in numbers. The sponsor, on the other hand, takes upon himself the responsibility for the growth and the welfare of the person he has sponsored.

PEOPLE WHO TREAT THEIR NETWORK AS NUMBERS NEVER SUCCEED IN THIS BUSINESS. TO SUCCEED YOU HAVE TO REMEMBER YOUR NETWORK CONSISTS OF HUMAN BEINGS WHO HAVE HOPES, DREAMS AND DESIRES. THEY HAVE INADEQUACIES, PROBLEMS AND FINANCIAL NEEDS. THEY NEED YOUR HELP TO SUCCEED. IF YOU ARE WILLING TO COACH AND HELP THEM WITH A SERVANT'S HEART, THEY WILL DELIVER RESULTS BEYOND YOUR WILDEST DREAMS!

What is the best way to develop a solid marketing force that never leaves your network? Sponsor a few key people at a time. Give them your full time and support. Build relationships. Help them to succeed in the business and train them to do the same. You have to build your network market on the right principles to succeed. There are no shortcuts. Are you willing to take the responsibility to become a sponsor? If so then, please read on.

There are people who will tell you "Just recruit a lot of distributors. You'll get at least a few good ones that way". Few leaders will emerge along the way, and your work is done. You can then have all the passive income you need. Leaders don't emerge in business. You have to find talent and develop them. Once in a while, you can get lucky, but that does not happen very often. You can't leave your business to chances if you wish to succeed.

The bottom line: *Leverage is mandatory for wealth creation, and you will NOT become wealthy without it. You are either exercising the power of leverage for yourself, or*

21

you are serving as leverage for someone else, and building their wealth for them.

To apply leverage, you have to find a network marketing company that has an exceptionally strong training and personal development program. Please look also at the credentials of the person who wishes to sponsor you. Is he committed to your success? Does your upline have requisite support systems for your training and success?

Avoid companies that boast of an automated recruiting system to increase numbers. You never build a network by merely having a recruiting system. Your network will collapse. To increase retention, you have to have a proper support organization and training that builds relationships. Do not join a company that focuses on recruiting and numbers.

Next important thing is that people must see a value in the product. Many network marketing companies fail because they do not have a product that can sustain the business. You can't fool people at all times. Network marketing is a relationship business that is built on good faith and recommendation. You just cannot build a strong belief system based on a weak product. Leverage can work only when retention rates are high.

Lastly and most importantly, people want a fair compensation for their effort in the business. There are network marketing companies that distribute only 10% to 30% of the total revenue to the distributors. There are companies that distribute over 50% of the Group Volume (GV) to their distributors. No wonder people stay in the business because they make money.

Some compensation plans are heavily loaded in favor of the 'heavy hitters' or the people who reach higher levels in the business. These plans do not adequately compensate the new distributors for their effort in the business. This results in new distributors getting disillusioned and dropping out. This is particularly bad for business.

For leveraging to work, retention is the golden key. To succeed in network marketing the business model or the compensation plan has to work correctly. The initial cost of joining the business, risk involved, return on investment (ROI), and the breakeven point has to be properly balanced out. The new distributors will stay in business if they can recoup their initial investment in the shortest possible time and start making a profit from the business.

Leveraging, which is the basic principle behind network marketing, can work only if the network you create has the power not only to sustain itself through high retention rate but also to expand itself exponentially once it is created and set up correctly. This can happen if there is the right kind of training and support systems, belief in the quality of the product and a fair, equitable and generous compensation plan in which new distributors can start earning money in the shortest possible time.

TRUTH # 6: You Will be Required to Spend Some Money in Order to Generate Money in Your Business. This is Regardless of What

You May Have Been Told. Ethical, Real and Legal Business is Not Free.

The majority of people out there will tell you that the only money you need is to enroll yourself, buy the products, use them and recommend them to others. Nothing can be further from the truth. If you want to succeed in network marketing, some money will be required to cover your travelling, communication and promotional costs. These like any other successful business need to be budgeted and recovered at the least possible time.

I agree that the startup cost for a network business is extremely low when compared to a traditional business because you work from home. You don't need to buy and keep stock. There is no need for warehousing or retail space. In most instances, the parent company gives you a back office to look at all the accounting details and order the products you need to sustain your business. However, you will need to promote your business if you are to succeed.

There are network marketing companies and affiliates who make millions of dollars selling promotional material to you at exorbitant costs. Their focus is on selling distributor kits and advertisement materials such as audio tapes, books, DVDs and brochures to their distributors. Many distributors fall prey to this and buy hundreds or even thousands of tapes at a time to use in mailings. Even in quantity, some of these companies charge reps $3 or $5 each for DVDs that cost 30¢ to duplicate! Such companies are driven by greed and ego. **They make a killing on the backs of their reps!**

You have to be extremely careful in not joining these companies. In most cases, such companies do not have a worthwhile product to sustain the sales. They then start generating money through the sale of promotional materials.

They will continually ask you to throw your hard-earned money to them. Please be warned of such companies. Legitimate expenses are OK if promotional materials are sold at a low cost or extremely low profit. The aim is to make money through the primary product and not the ancillary promotional materials. When the focus shifts to make money from the promotional products then the company and you as their business partner are bound to fail.

Promotion is crucial to the success of your business. It is critical how much money you spend towards promoting your business. Each dollar spent in promotion must have a tangible outcome for your business or you will go bust.

Later in the book, we shall see how to budget your business and how to expand fast on low cost but effective marketing methods. It will be explained how to maintain cash flow to sustain your business. You will also learn on how to reach breakeven and to earn profit in the shortest possible time.

TRUTH #7: Creating A Successful Income Producing Network Marketing Business is Not Anywhere Close to As "EASY OR EFFORTLESS" As It Appears.

There are people who will tell you "WE'LL BUILD YOUR DOWNLINE FOR YOU!" or "WE HAVE AN AUTOMATED SYSTEM THAT WILL RECRUIT WITHOUT ANY EFFORT FROM YOU"

You may have come across programs promising an easy way to recruit associates. These programs suggest ways that guarantee success for yourself and the people you recruit. When you've read their material, you perhaps would have thought it was virtually impossible for *anyone* to fail. If you have been in any of these programs, please see your commission check. It will never lie.

There is no recruiting system that can do the entire job by itself. On a legitimate program, there is no money in just recruiting people. No matter how clever the computer program or how exciting the compensation plan looks, there is work to be done if you have to succeed.

NO BUSINESS CAN BE EVER BUILD AUTOMATICALLY WITHOUT ANY EFFORT FROM YOU. IF SOMEONE IS SUGGESTING THAT THEY HAVE AN INCOME OPPORTUNITY THAT CAN "DO IT ALL" FOR YOU THEN RUN AWAY AS FAST AND AS FAR AS YOU CAN BEFORE YOU LOSE YOUR MONEY.

There is no such thing as a 'Millionaires Free party'. Nobody is going to FILL UP your bank account out of goodwill! There were people who came to me and offer me opportunities in which I don't have to do anything at all ... not even advertise. "We will do it all FOR you..." they said. This is like running a car without gas. Ask yourself this question, and answer it honestly: "Can anyone make you rich without you doing anything at all?" If you are struggling with the answer to that question, I can help you. The answer is a **BIG NO**.

There are MLM companies especially on the internet who make such preposterous claims. They appeal to your greediness and lazy human nature. Try to go back after one year and find these companies. They've vanished with your money into thin air without a trace. So, please beware.

If creating a network marketing business from scratch is anywhere near as easy, effortless or inexpensive as many "gurus" attempt to make it appear, we would be earning million dollar of passive income every year. So get real! Roll up your sleeves and get to work. *There is BIG money to be made but you have to work for it. The BIG difference is that, the money you will generate is a PASSIVE income for life.* You will just work once and get paid over and over. Your effort will be rewarded for a lifetime. This is an intelligent work.

People spend a fortune and years getting trained to become doctors and engineers. They then get into jobs that pay them by the hour with little or no long term security. Even if you just put a quarter of that time and effort, you can still build an unimaginable amount of passive income. This will give you and your family a lifetime of financial security.

Please read correctly: **NETWORK MARKETING** and you will never go wrong.

TRUTH# 8: It Takes Time In Network Marketing Business To Make BIG MONEY.

There is no chance of making any money in the network marketing business if you throw the towel after just a few weeks or maybe months of not receiving favorable results. It takes time to master any sort of techniques that will bring you income. People who go "opportunity hopping" rather than to commit to learn on how to market one opportunity correctly will remain broke.

I met many "network marketers" who gave up opportunities when they met the slightest amount of problems. They want to make easy money. They jump from one opportunity to another hoping that they will hit a gold mine. They continue to sing the same song and dance the same dance, each time with a NEW company name behind their act? The truth is-- such people have ZERO INTEGRITY.

By 'opportunity hopping', these people sabotage their OWN ability to make money regardless of what business opportunity they join. They also confuse the people whom they sponsor with their uncertain state of mind. Either you have to be consistent or learn to accept being broke.

NETWORK MARKETING WORKS ON COMPOUNDING PRINCIPLE.

UNFORTUNATELY, MOST PEOPLE DO NOT COMPREHEND HOW THE POWER OF COMPOUNDING ACTUALLY WORKS.

Albert Einstein, one of the finest minds in the history of mankind, once remarked, ***"One of the most amazing phenomenon of our universe is the power of compounding"***. It is equally remarkable that so few fully understand either its power or application.

For easier understanding let us take an example. Suppose you start your network marketing business by sponsoring one person in the first month. Imagine too that you teach/help this person to sponsor another person. Let us say this teaching and sponsoring process takes one month. In a month or two, if you personally sponsor one more person and the person whom you sponsored in the first month also sponsors another person then you will have 4 people in your team. In the 3rd month, you will have 8 persons in your team through sponsoring and training. If the same process is repeated month after month, your organization will grow in the following manner:

Month 1: You + 1 = 2

Month2: 2 +2 = 4

Month3: 4+4 = 8

Month 4: 8+8 = 16

Month 5: 16+16 = 32

Month 6: 32+32 = 64

Month 7: 64+64 = 128

Month8: 128+128 = 256

Month9: 256+256 = 512

Month10: 512+512 =1024

Month 11: 1024+1024 = 2048

Month12: 2048+2048 = 4096

If you observe the table you will find that, after three months, your team has only 8 members. Nothing exciting. You might be subsiding your purchases. But wait......in sixth months, your organization will grow to 64. You will be earning a little money to sustain your interests but, NO BIG DEAL. Your life and financial future have not changed.

On completion of 9 months, your team has now grown to 512. Now for the first time, you are seeing the fruits of your labor. There is a renewed understanding that the business actually works. And the fun continues ...... in the 12th month your organization is taking a life of its own. It has now grown to 4096. Each member of your team is trying to secure his/her financial future.

Your organization is not only big but growing at a faster rate without much effort from you. Your passive income is flowing in ever greater amounts each month. You feel rich for the first time in your life. The essential fact is that, during the 12 month period, you have only sponsored 12 people into the business and trained them to conduct the business properly. The remainder of your network has been created through the power of leverage.

In the first month, your organization had just two people in it. In the twelfth month, it grew by 2048 people for the same effort on your part. This is the phenomenal power of compounding in network marketing.

If compounding and growing a network is so easy then why don't most people succeed? The reason is exceedingly straightforward, but most people don't get it .... ***The power of networking and compounding takes time to take effect.***

The Tunnelling Effect

In network marketing, when you are starting out, all the hard work takes place upfront. You have nothing to show for your effort. This is called the 'Tunneling Effect'. There is darkness all around and a little hope. This is where most people give up because they do not see any results for their sacrifice, hard work and effort.

Most people who joined the network marketing came from jobs where they are paid by the hour. They are accustomed seeing a direct correlation between the hours they work and the compensation they receive. If they work 5 hours, then they expect 5 hours pay.

In a network marketing business, one has to think like an entrepreneur. When an entrepreneur starts a business, there is a gestation period. He knows that profits will flow in due course of time if the business is set up correctly.

An entrepreneur works one hundred hours and gets no payment. Once the business is set up, he can work five hours and gets paid for a thousand hours.

For employed people who enter network marketing have to go through a shift in mental attitude. Initially, network marketing does not pay you by the hour. If one is full of patience and perseverance at this stage, then there is not only light at the end of the tunnel but full glory of the sun. Anyone who became rich has passed through this dark tunnel. There is no escaping it.

In network marketing, you have to learn and teach people to take a long-time approach to the growth of their business. It takes time to grow organizations. It takes time to create depth and ongoing duplication. It takes time to develop a team and create serious residual income. Those who can develop and maintain a mindset of an entrepreneur understand this and succeed. Those who fail to grasp this simple truth fail in this business.

IN NETWORK MARKETING YOU ARE LIKE A ROCKET THAT BURNS 90% OF ITS FUEL AT THE TAKE OFF STAGE. ONCE YOU ARE IN ORBIT IT IS A CRUISE CONTROL. IT WILL TAKE TIME AND EFFORT ON YOUR PART TO SUSTAIN AND GROW YOUR BUSINESS IN THE INITIAL STAGES.

Warren Buffet, one of the richest men in the world, remarked about his wife when he was building his wealth "***Susie didn't get very excited when I told her we were going to get rich. She*** *either didn't care or didn't believe me - probably both, in fact.*" You can read the biography of any wealth creator, and you will find in it the universal truth of the 'tunneling effect' and how they wanted to quit but didn't. In network marketing, you will never make it if you quit before you reach the critical mass. That's where the real fun starts.

Critical Mass

If you persist and as time goes by-- the critical mass kicks in and things get better. Your network becomes self-perpetuating. It starts growing under its own steam. The challenge at this stage is not to change course. **The problem with the human mind is that, it loses focus remarkably quickly. It gets attracted to other thought and ideas and will start looking at other options. The key here is to maintain focus**.

Compounding is boring -- b-o-r-i-n-g. It is boring until the money starts to pour in. Then, believe me, compounding becomes very interesting. In fact, it becomes downright fascinating! Compounding if allowed to continue will take your wealth to unlimited levels.

Ninety percent of the people dropped out from network marketing because they do not fully appreciate the power of compounding. They get discouraged when they faced the tunneling effect and quit. They don't understand that light is just around the corner. **Dogged persistence is a great quality** to have if you want to succeed.

Compounding Only Works through Time

The great thing about network compounding is that anyone can do it. Compounding is the royal road to building your network. To compound successfully, you need the following: **perseverance** in order to keep you firmly on the path of creating a successful network. You need **time**, time to allow the power of compounding network to work for you. Remember, compounding *only works through time. **Time, in fact, is the most powerful element in the process of compounding.*** **Nothing comes close to it.**

It takes time, effort, practice and patience to become skilled at network marketing and build a business. Don't quit when the success is around the corner. Above all, stay *FOCUSED.*

TRUTH# 9: Ninety Percent of the Time When People Fail in Network Marketing the Fault Is With the Network Marketer Rather Than the Product or the Company

The wind of fortune blows evenly on everyone. It is the same wind that strikes the sail of each one of us. People who are skilled and know how to trim their sail reach their destination safely and in the shortest possible time. On the other hand, people who lack the basic skills do not how to make use of the winds of fortune will get lost in the wilderness and never reach their destination.

This is the reason why some people succeed in network marketing whilst others fail with the same product, company, support system and the compensation plan. The reason is simple........it is not the opportunity that is the problem; it is the lack of skills to make use of the opportunity.

A bad workman always complains about his tools. This is very true about network marketing. People who fail in network marketing always complain about the company, the product, their upline support......... *THE PROBLEM IS ALWAYS THE NETWORK MARKETER.*

BLAME, BLAME, BLAME.................EXCUSES, EXCUSES, EXCUSES......... They live below the line....... they never look at themselves as the cause of failure. If they look closer at their own attitude then they will understand why they failed.

Network Marketing is a great concept. Hundreds of thousands of people are making a fortune out of this opportunity. Robert Kiyosaki calls it the perfect business because ***it allows people to shift from employee/ self-employed mind set to the business quadrant mindset.*** This is the first crucial step towards financial success. In network marketing, the startup costs and risks are extremely low as compared to a traditional business. The returns, on the other hand, can be as high as a big business. So it is not the business concept or opportunity that is a failure. In most cases, it is the network marketeer who is the real problem.

Majority of the people fail in this business because of lack of belief in the network marketing model. They fail because they lack the belief that they can succeed. They fail because they are unable to make a shift from the mentality of an employee or self-employed to that of running a business.

They take advice from their friends, brother-in-law or Uncle Tom about the business opportunity. They do not speak with the people who are successful in the business. They keep company of those who are failures in life. They are not teachable and not willing to learn or be mentored by successful people in the business.

Such people will hop from one opportunity to another- they are chasing the rainbows. They want easy and quick money without any effort on their part. They can have the best product or opportunity in the world yet remain broke if they don't take the effort to educate themselves in the art of network marketing and believe that they can succeed.

You succeed in network marketing when you are willing to take responsibility for your business. If you keep waiting for your upline to build your business, it will never happen. If you look at your tree in the network, you will find your position is at the very top. You are the CEO of your business. You have to be a leader to lead your team. The moment you assume the mantle of responsibility, your business will succeed.

The problem with network marketing is that there is loss of knowledge as it filters down the organization. Person A sponsors person B into the organization. A has 100% knowledge regarding the product, company and network marketing business. He mentors B who manages to absorb only 75% of the knowledge. Now B sponsors C and mentors him. C absorbs only 50% of the information. When it comes to D, there is a huge problem because he gets to know only 25% of the knowledge.

To overcome this problem, each person in the organization has to take responsibility for upgrading his or her knowledge by getting information from more than one source. Later in the book I will show you how we can overcome this problem so that the best quality training can be imparted without any loss of knowledge.

Most people who join the network marketing industry literally have no clue on how to do marketing. I am dead serious. Please don't take that personally because I'm not trying to offend anyone. It's just the truth. (Most of the time it's just that people are unaware of what they're doing and what they're teaching others to do).

Why is this? It's because network marketing is a business that's designed for the "average person". 95% of people who get involved in network marketing have no real foundation in effective sales and marketing. The stuff they pass on to their equally unknowing team members can only be described as pure garbage.

To succeed, you have to take some time, effort, patience and practice. You have to learn. You have to make a mental shift. You have to be mentored. Above all, you have to ACT. If you do all this you will start having small successes along the way.

In time, you will have more success. This will start building your belief system and your business will explode. It is always the first step to succeed that is very crucial. The first step has to be in the right direction. These are small building blocks that have the power to change your destiny. This is not a miracle business. On the other hand, it is a very simple business. It is so simple that anyone can do it. The only hitch is that it starts with you...........Are you willing to take the challenge?

TRUTH# 10: To Succeed In Network Marketing You Have To Learn the Art of Selling

This appears to be something different from what I said earlier wherein network marketing is not a direct sales business but a mentoring and relationship business. I hold the statement to be true, but it is in relation to the emphasis on direct sales in network marketing. Selling, when seen in a larger context is a very important ingredient to succeed in life. There is a thin line that you need to understand.

People lie to you when they say that there is no selling involved in network marketing. So at the time of sponsoring, they will put a smoke screen and deceive you that there is no selling involved. This is because most people hate to sell. They fear rejection that is associated with selling. They would run away if they have to sell anything. They don't want to hear the truth and, therefore, they are told lies.

The truth is, **'Selling'** *is the most important life skill you need if you want to be rich and successful'*. Money is only when you sell an idea, product, or service in the market place. Without selling, there is no money or success. In fact, selling and promoting is required in every aspect of your life if you want to succeed.

When you go to a job interview, you have to sell your job skills and personality. You have to continuously promote yourself and your ideas to get recognition and promotion in life. Even in attracting a member of the opposite sex, you need to sell your beauty, charm and virtues. Most people do these things subconsciously, but the smart ones understand the importance of mastering the art of selling and promotion to get ahead in life.

"What make people rich are skills. And the number one skill of an entrepreneur is the ability to sell."

- ROBERT KIYOSAKI

This is a blunt truth that you have to understand if you want to succeed in network marketing. You have to master the art of selling, the concept of network marketing and also to promote your company and products.

Building relationship and mentoring are important parts of your promotion. People should believe that you can support them in their effort to succeed. You have to sell and promote yourself to be a leader.

SELL! Sell, sell, sell, sell is a four-letter word. That's the word everybody's afraid of! But? Sales = _Income._

99% of the time people fail in network marketing because they have been told at the onset that no selling is involved. This is partly true because no direct sales are required to succeed in network marketing. They still need to sell the concept, the strength of their company and product. Above all, they have to sell themselves so that others have the confidence to join the team. Most people become a victim of the lie that no selling is required, and they teach the same lies unknowingly to the people they sponsor. Without SELLING, there is NO BUSINESS and no wonder they do not succeed in the network marketing effort.

To succeed you have to be honest to the people you sponsor. Even if you teach them some basic marketing and selling skills, their chances of success will improve a hundred fold. If they go around with the belief that no selling is involved, they will surely fail.

Chapter 3

THE SMART WAY

In life, there is the hard way, and there is the SMART way. Most of us are only familiar with the hard way, and that is why financial freedom never becomes a reality. If you do network marketing the right way, then it is possible to replace your current income in six to eighteen months' time and be financially free in two to three years. The next part of this book will reveal how to do network marketing the right way.

The first step to your success is to choose the right company.

SMART WAY #1: CHOOSE THE RIGHT OPPORTUNITY

Majority of people choose an opportunity without any research. This is because you are approached by a family or friend about a business opportunity and you joined because of your love and trust in the relationship. In 99% of the cases, the person who is sponsoring you has done no due diligence regarding the company. It is like blind pushing the blind. The result is invariably a catastrophe.

Remember what you are getting into, is a business. It is about money. It is about your time, effort and sweat. It is about your future and the future of your loved ones. It depends upon the quality of your decision. So, please choose carefully and intelligently.

THE COMPANY YOU CHOOSE MUST HAVE THE MANAGEMENT WITH RIGHT EXPERIENCE AND INTEGRITY

This is very important. The reason why Warren Buffet is the most successful investor is because when he buys stocks of a company he looks at the men behind the company. It is always people behind the company who are the wealth creators. If the management is weak or lacks integrity, the business will fail. So when you decide to join a network marketing company, do some research first on the people behind the company?

It is the distributors who are the real stars of the company. If the distributors are not present the company will have no sales. Yet, there are companies who look to compensation plans that increase the company profits at the expense of the distributors. They look to create breaks in the compensation plan so that they can stop paying distributors if they become too successful.

People join network marketing companies to create residual income. However, when they wish to retire, some companies feel like 'why should we continue paying them if they are doing no work?' So they look for ways and means to terminate the contract. They insert clauses in the fine print of terms and conditions (which nobody reads at the time of becoming a distributor) that the company has the right to terminate the contract if there is no ongoing sales or sponsoring, or if the person does not attend the company sponsored meetings. Sometimes, they reserve the right to terminate the contract without assigning any reasons at all.

Companies also add a clause that you can't be a part of class action lawsuit. In other words, you can't even sue them if they terminate your contract. This is like someone taking away the income that you've achieved through a lifetime of work. It is an outright stealing. Such actions speak of very low integrity. Never become part of such a company. Read the fine print in terms and conditions before signing up to become a distributor.

The management must have the experience to take the company to a new level as the business grows. They must have the ability to guide the company during hard times. If the company fails to adapt and survive the changing times and economic conditions, so are you. If the company performs, well then your business will grow exponentially.

Integrity and experience of management is very important to your success, and you should never compromise this aspect when selecting a company to join.

TIMING IN JOINING A BUSINESS IS OF GREAT ESSENCE. YOU CAN EITHER RIDE THE WAVE TO SUCCESS OR BE DROWNED BY IT

Right timing consists of two separate factors and these should not be confused. First, is the right timing in the industry. Second factor is the right timing in the company. We will discuss them in details. If you get one right and the other wrong, then you will not get great results. If you get both the timings right, then you will ride the wave of success.

TIMING IN THE INDUSTRY

Each industry has a cycle. Some product cycles are very long while other product cycles are very short. For instance, few years back, there was great excitement regarding video emails. Some network marketing companies called it the wave of the future and started enrolling distributors. Today, video emailing is free on the internet. What happened to the profit margins of these companies? Obviously, they never survived. What happened to all the effort by the distributors? ZERO outcome. They lost their time, effort and money in promoting a product that has just a life span of two to three years only.

This doesn't mean that you should avoid technology companies. Many internet companies have the technological edge and can give you a very high residual cash flow within a very short frame of time.

High technology products have very high returns but relatively short window of opportunity. So when you join a technology/ internet company, you have to access the life of the products and enter the business at the right time.

To succeed in network marketing is to be in an industry that preferably has a long product cycle that will not go out of fashion or become redundant with technological change. The most successful products in the network marketing business have been those related to the health and wellness industry. These products are timeless, as the need to live longer, look younger and be healthier will always remain. It is the basic human need. It will never go out of style.

The timing for health products is also perfect with baby boomers coming of age in their late fifties and sixties. For the last six decades, baby boomers had determined the industry trends. In the next two decades, the main concern of the baby boomers will be their health. Health, which is a $20 billion dollar industry today, is expected to explode to trillion dollars in sales on the wave of the baby boomers by 2020. Timing, therefore determines when to join network marketing companies promoting health products. The big wave is set to go into motion, and we should ride this 'health' wave or we will miss a great opportunity in history.

When the timing is right, NON-network marketers will take your product to the marketplace. The timing means NOW. Not 4 years earlier, not 4 years later. Timing will make your work ten times easier. Millionaires were made in network marketing because of timing alone. Learn to ride the wave!

One warning though about the health industry before you rush to join. The retention rate in this industry is around 6% to 8%. It may be slightly higher if you have a very strong training program in place. This is because profit margins when compared to internet-based opportunities are much lower. It also takes far greater effort to build a network in a non-digital product company.

In some of the internet-based companies that I am involved with, my retention rate of affiliates is over 90%. This is because my affiliates make money very soon after joining the business.

Nothing is permanent in life. Each and every product has a life cycle. You have to weigh the product life cycle, profitability and retention rates of affiliates before deciding on which company to join.

TIMING IN THE COMPANY

Once you have selected the industry, then you have to look for a company within the industry whose timing is right for you to join. How can you gauge the timing in a company? It is difficult, but below are some tips:

Most companies fail in the first year or two of their operations. You'll waste a lot of time, money & energy if you get in too early.

B. You'll waste a lot of time, money & energy if you get in too late. Momentum growth period of these companies occurred years ago. These companies are household names maybe with products using out dated technology. They are like dinosaurs facing extinction. You will fight a real uphill financial battle to sponsor people into these companies.

The best time to join a company is around 3-5 years for physical products and 1-3 years for internet-based companies upon their start up. By the time, it has proven its staying power and about go into momentum growth.

If you can get the timing of the industry and the company right, and also the other parts of the formula correctly, then you are perfectly positioned to ride the momentum wave to wealth.

THE PRODUCT HAS TO BE REMARKABLE

If there is no EMOTIONAL attachment to the product, you will not succeed. You can never recommend a product to someone if you are not emotionally involved with it. Network marketing is a referral-based marketing. You can never transfer your enthusiasm to someone if you don't have feelings for the product.

Network marketing works with niche quality products that have special qualities that need to be sold through transference of knowledge and enthusiasm. Network marketing does not work with ordinary products that have little or no intrinsic value.

When you promote multiple of opportunities and products, you undermine your network. If you try to appeal to everybody with your multiple streams of products & services, no one will take you seriously. This is because you have failed to create an identity in their mind. The net result is...

No trust. No loyalty. No network.

Loss Of focus = Loss Of Power. You ruin your quality perception, because to consumers, *Specializing = Quality*. You will struggle to market numerous unrelated services and products that you don't know well. You lose competitiveness and efficiency, and as a result, you will get a smaller market share. You better do your research! Choose the RIGHT opportunity and product, and FOCUS ON THAT ONE!

If you are focused, you will attract the customers & associates you want. They will be excited because they feel that they are a part of something big. It will create a belief in their minds that you'll be a big success. **A specialist always knows more and so as better quality product always wins over hundreds of mediocre products and services**. You will win if you remain focused in a quality niche market.

The product has to be so remarkable that people should be willing to buy it even if there is no compensation plan involved. The product has to be priced right. If you start explaining why the product is so expensive, then you will become a salesperson rather than a network marketer.

In any network marketing organization, there will be around 80% of the people who are users only of the product and will never build the business. If the product is not remarkable or priced correctly, then these people will stop using the product.

The business simply cannot succeed if people do not find a great value in the product.

The product should not be readily available in the super markets and neighborhood stores. It does not make sense for someone to buy a product that can be bought cheaper from a store next door. The product has to be unique and remarkable. The product has to be difficult to replicate. If everyone starts replicating the product then the price starts to go down, and the margins get squeezed out. The company will go out of business and so are you.

Most importantly, the product should be a consumable type that people use it every day and they need to buy it every week or month. In this case, if there are no volumes in product sales/consumption, then there will be no income.

THE COMPENSATION PLAN MUST BE EQUITABLE, JUST AND WORK WITH NUMBERS

The most important thing about a compensation plan is that it should work with numbers. If it works for only 5% of the people and not for the other 95%, then the compensation plan will not succeed.

The business plan has to be equitable and just. Newly sponsored people will remain in the network, only if they see the plan working for them. They should not only break-even but be in profit within the shortest possible time.

You can lead people, only if you can take them one step closer to their dreams. You have to show them small successes before they are prepared to take the long march with you. You are doomed from the very start if the plan does not work with numbers. The plan has to work for average or ordinary people.

This is because most people who join your business are in the average and ordinary level.

The business plan has to work for average part-time workers who make the numbers. **If the plan does not work with numbers, then simply walk away.**

Network marketing statistics show that an average distributor sponsors 2.7 persons into their home business. This means that *any compensation plan that requires more than 3 persons in their frontline will struggle to survive.* **Binary plans that require only two persons to be put in the front line have proved to be most successful in the industry.**

Any successful network marketer will tell you that the main source of his income in network marketing comes from two to three people in his team. If this be the case, then compensation plans that are too wide just do not work. Binary plans cause spillovers that support the effort of the new members in the team.

The new members feel great when their upline places someone below them in their team. This helps build relationships that are essential in network marketing. Always choose a plan that does not force you to go wide and rewards you to work deep. Working in depth helps create a relationship with your team members.

Any compensation plan that rewards recruiting into the system is illegal. Most likely, such plans are illegal pyramids with no tangible product in the offing. In illegal pyramids, the moment you stop recruiting, your income will stop. Such companies camouflage their intentions by selling products that have little or no value. Sooner or later, authorities will close down these companies for illegal practices. You should never become part of such scams and lose your hard earned money and effort.

For a network marketing company to be ethical and legal, the money in the compensation plan has to flow out from the sale of products. The joining fee for such companies is normally very low because there is no money to be made from sponsoring people. This helps in sponsoring new people into the business because the startup cost is very low. Ethical companies succeed on the basis of a strong product that people want to buy and use.

A good business plan should be backed by a generous contribution from the company for the efforts put in by the distributors. *A method to check if the compensation by the company is really generous is to check how many people need to be in your network to generate an income of $10,000 per month.* If the figure runs into thousands of distributors, then it will take a long time for you to generate any decent income. There are companies who only give back 15% to 25% of the turnover to the distributors. You will put in twice the amount of effort to build your business compared to a company that pays out 40% to 50% of the sales turnover.

Another important feature of a compensation plan is that the points are non-flushing. As long as you are active in the business, your group volume points should never be lost and will carry forward week to week until such time you qualify for commissions. This is a big advantage compared to many compensation plans wherein your points get flushed out at the end of the month if you don't qualify for commissions.

Publicly-traded companies have the advantage as the details of their finances are available for public scrutiny. On the other hand, they suffer the disadvantage of high operating costs when compared to privately-held companies. These costs get added to the price of the product, and as a result, the compensation paid to the distributors gets squeezed out.

Privately-held companies operate with much lower overheads and can take business decisions more quickly. This makes them more profitable. However, you will find it difficult to learn about the state of their finances as these companies are not obliged to go public with this information.

CHOOSE AN OPPOPTUNITY WITH SYSTEMS FOR DUPLICATION

Why most businesses fail, is because they do not have systems in place. On the other hand, businesses with mediocre products but with great business systems always succeed. Take the example of McDonald's. They do not make the best burger in the business. Even your mom will make a better burger. McDonald's is the largest burger chain in the world simply because it has the best business system.

This is also true for network marketing companies. Check the business systems of a company before you decide to join them. Go for a system that respects people and attracts like-minded individuals.

To succeed in this business, you need a proven and tested duplication system. The system has to be very simple, or it will not be duplicated by ordinary members of your team. Everyone that you sponsor and those they sponsor need a step-by-step system to get their business off to a fast start. These systems can be online, offline, one-on-one, or in cold market, warm market, retailing, recruiting or becoming a mentor to their personally-sponsored people.

The system must also help to develop the individual members and build leadership. A person does not need all the techniques to be successful but the system should make these available to choose from that is best suited for his style of business.

To the best of my knowledge, there is no company in network marketing that provides a comprehensive, realistic and affordable system to help you build your business. This is because it is the job of the network marketer to build his own business that is best suited to his style. The company provides you the backup system so that stocking, distribution and customer complaints/queries are taken care of. They pay you generously to spread the word and bring in new customers.

Every company has individual groups of entrepreneurial reps who put in place a system to help you build your business. You cannot succeed without the help of these people and the support systems they provide. If you want to leverage your time and effort you have to join one of these groups to succeed. They help not only you but the people you sponsor into the business. Don't join a group unless they have such a system in place.

There is a book I have written on this important subject of '*How to Find a Network Marketing Goldmine: Researching and Evaluating MLM Opportunities*' **that you might like to read.**

SMART WAY# 2: BUILDING BUSINESS THE RIGHT WAY

Successful network marketing works on this simple model given below:

A. Number of LEADS you can generate.

B. Number of LEADS you can CONVERT into your team.

C. Quality of mentoring and training you can give to your TEAM members regarding the products, business systems and promotions. This will start the DUPLICATION process.

D. Help new member to be in profit within the shortest possible time to help increase the retention rate.

E. Develop leadership within the team.

These are five essential steps to your success in network marketing. Most people struggle, because they do not understand the five steps clearly. If, through our training process, we teach you how to improve on your performance by simple 20% in each of these five areas, your business will explode exponentially. People suffer in this business because of ignorance. If you are teachable and learn a few simple things, then you have a huge advantage over a normal network marketer. Your success is guaranteed.

Let us examine these five simple steps one by one.

LEAD GENERATION THE RIGHT WAY

Leads are the life blood of your business. Without leads, you are nowhere. There are two distinct schools of thought here. The warm market leads and leads generated through advertising. Let us examine them at some length because this is very important.

WARM MARKET LEADS

There are very successful network marketers who have built huge businesses only through warm market leads. Warm market leads have some distinct advantages. Firstly, there is already an ongoing relationship of trust. Network marketing is a relationship business. To succeed, you have to build a special relationship of trust with the person you sponsor.

In warm market leads, the relationship already exists and makes your job easier. Secondly it is easier to share your excitement about a product, service or business with someone you already know than with a total stranger. This transference of excitement and sharing of joy is very important in building your network marketing business.

Network marketing works on recommendations and the person who most likely will listen to your recommendations is someone who already knows and trusts you. Most importantly, your warm market leads don't cost you a dime. Advertising can be very expensive, and you can max out your credit cards yet still not did not reach your target audience.

The problem with warm market leads is the poor conversion rate. This is because you are talking with leads that are not looking for a business opportunity. For most of these leads timing may not be right. Some may be going through change of jobs, transfers, shift of residence, new arrivals in the family and other family issues.

A NO from your dear ones hurts and you feel rejected. The NO can spring from lots of reasons totally unrelated to the business opportunity, and it is definitely not a rejection of you as a person as long as you don't pester them and make them feel uncomfortable. You have every right to share your enthusiasm for a product and/or an idea. There is no reason to be upset if they are closed to your idea.

Network marketing has been given a bad name by some people who will not take NO for an answer. They will badger their contacts with the hope of wearing them down and change their minds. Please remember, everyone will not be as excited about the opportunity as you are because the timing may not be right for them.

You discuss the opportunity with the next person in the list. It is recommended that you make a very long list. A short list will create problem. As you start making money, and your belief in the business goes up, you will find a sudden change in the attitude of your warm market. You will find it very easy to convert them to your cause. People, who initially said NO, will want to join the business. This is how the business works. You have to remain calm, consistent and focused regardless of the views of your warm market in the initial stages of your business.

DO NOT TRY AND CONVINCE.......JUST SHOW THE OPPORTUNITY TO MAXIMUM NUMBER OF PEOPLE YOU KNOW. You will win if you take MASSIVE, CONSISTENT and PERSISTENT ACTION

The key to succeed with your WARM MARKET is to start them on the products, and not pitch the opportunity to them straight away! Once you get your family and friends try the products *(it won't cost you that much considering that you can claim tax breaks)*, and once they see results from it, they will start buying and promoting the products to the people around them because of the benefit they experienced! Some may even join the business opportunity!

You can never run out of warm leads. Once you have sponsored a few people into the business, you have to start supporting them and working through their leads. Sooner than later you will find active network marketeers who share the same vision as you and your business starts growing.

COLD MARKET LEADS THROUGH ADVERTISEMENTS

The leads you generate through online and offline advertisement are highly-motivated leads. These people are searching for home businesses. They will look at various options before deciding on the best opportunity. The conversion rates from these leads can be fairly high. You can build your business very rapidly through advertising. The best part of it? There is very little or no rejection factor as in the case of warm leads.

One thing I can warn you from the very start is to *NEVER EVER BUY LEADS* because these leads are sold over and over again. The only thing you will achieve is to pay for these expensive leads with no returns to your business. *To be successful in the business, you have to generate your own leads.* There are no SHORTCUTS.

The problem of leads through advertising is not only the prohibitive cost but also skills needed to reach the target audience. If you choose the advertising route, you will be competing against big companies for attention.

If your advertisements are not focused and targeted, they will not reach the right people. Either you have to become a master at marketing which includes developing great writing skills in advertising, knowing the right medium to advertise in order to gain maximum impact and also know how to monitor the cost returns on advertising.

Without proper monitoring systems in place, you will blow up your budget without any tangible returns. If you are advertising on the internet, then you have to develop special skills to market on the internet. Most average people do not have the necessary skills to advertise effectively, and if you are one of them, then you can spend thousands of dollars and achieve very little or no results.

There are unscrupulous upline leaders who will ask their members to embark on expensive advertising to grow their business even when they don't have specialized knowledge to guide their team.

Another problem with generating leads through advertisements is that there is no relationship with the lead. To succeed, you have to build a relationship of trust. This takes time and effort. The problem is compounded because the leads that you generate may not be from your local area. You have to set up systems for long distance support by taking advantage of the modern day communications and the internet. The support systems have to go in place before you start to advertise. You will need to budget the additional website and communication costs.

There is no doubt that **advertisement can greatly help your business to grow rapidly, but you have to master the art to succeed**. If you are a beginner, it is advisable to stick to the warm market leads until such time you reach the breakeven point in your business and you are in profit. You can then start slowly by advertising first using free resources.

There are various avenues of free advertising, and we shall discuss some of them later in this book. As your income from business grows, and skills improve, you can slowly start experimenting with paid advertising. Remember, every dollar you spend on advertising must be monitored. You should have positive results in building your business or you are simply wasting money.

The most effective leads you can generate for your business is through internet marketing. If you are not using the internet to generate leads, then you should start doing so without delay. The best part is that you do not need paid advertising to generate leads on the internet. You can use social media, even article and video marketing to generate leads for free.

MyLeadsSytemPro is one of the best programs on the internet that teaches you how to generate leads and position you as a market leader. It is based on the principles of attraction marketing and funded proposal. Attraction marketing was first propounded by Mike Dillard through his book and Magnetic Sponsoring system.

According to attraction marketing, you should not chase people into joining your business. You have to position yourself as a market leader so that others want to follow your prosperity model and join your business.

Funded proposal means that you make money from leads that do not join your business to cover the costs of your advertising. Let us say it costs you $1 to generate a lead. Most of the leads that you generate will not join your primary business as it may not be suitable for them or they may be engaged in another business from which they do not wish to shift their focus. The advertising money that you have spent will be a loss to you.

If there is a way for you to sell some products to these leads to help them with their business effort, then you will not only recover your advertising costs but also make a small profit. Let us say that you earn $3 from every lead you generate through your marketing system that costs you $1. This small profit will enable you to scale up your advertising budget progressively. This is what MyLeadsSytemPro is designed to do for your business.

For someone new to the business, the best option is to first work with the warm market leads. Next step is to generate leads by adverting through FREE resources. Paid advertising should be attempted after having gained the necessary skills in setting up the organization for long distance support and once the business is in profit. The only exception to this rule is if you already have expertise in advertising or have deep pockets to hire an expert.

SMART WAY# 3: JUMP START THROUGH HIGHER COVERSION RATE

Converting leads into team members is a function of your BELIEF that you have in your product, compensation plan, integrity of your company and the network marketing concept of wealth creation. We have covered this in details earlier. If you have the **BELIEF THAT YOU CAN SUCCEED AND ARE WILLING TO LEAD........ CONVERSION RATE WILL GO THROUGH THE ROOF.**

Conversion rate also depends on your skill level. **MLM is first and foremost a people business.** So, the first thing you have to master is the people skills. **Spend your time studying people ... and learn how to find the people STARVING for what you have to offer.** *FIND A MOB OF STARVING PEOPLE*

AND THEY WILL CONVERT TO YOUR CAUSE WITH MINIMUM EFFORT.

If you do not understand what the prospect is looking for, then you will never be able to sponsor the person. You must learn to discover the dreams that shape and drive a person. <u>If a person is not aware of his dreams</u>, <u>help him to uncover the dreams. Don't talk too much........just listen to their dreams</u>. What do they want most passionately? How do their desires drive them in decision-makings? What gets them in frenzy when they look for an opportunity?

What attracts them? Is it your product or your compensation plan? If a person is attracted to your product, don't drive him away by focusing on the business plan. Network marketing is not recruiting. It is relating.

"Why Do Some People Succeed in Network Marketing, While Others NEVER Do?"

The answer to this simple question is that, successful people make the effort to understand what really makes people tick ... what motivates them ... why they make the choices.

Research has shown that there are four distinct types of personalities. It is called the **DISC Personality** composition. *D stands for Dominance, I for Influence, S for Submission and C for Compliance*. Understanding the DISC personality and how to deal with them will greatly improve the ratio of conversion.

DISC TO SUCCESS

DOMINANCE or 'D'

DOMINANCE or 'D' is 15% of the population. They relate to control, power and assertiveness. They are motivated by money and are money-focused.

Don't bother talking to them about family and social things. They don't care. They are ambitious, determined, egocentric and strong-willed.

How to Sponsor a 'D'

All they want to talk about is money, money and money. They think network marketing is a sales business. For them, it is sell, sell, sell. They're just looking for somebody who will build, build, build. They are happy with 5% retentions. For them, it's a sales business.

'Ds' are the corporate CEOs. They are "get-the-job-done" type of people who believe that everyone in network marketing is trying to recruit them. But it's a fallacy. You simply cannot coach them.

They have big egos. They like to order people around. It works in the corporate world, but not in network marketing. They can drive people away.

You want to sponsor 'Ds' because they have the connections and will put you in contact with the right kind of people who matter. They know business owners and leaders. Don't ever try to coach or mentor them. Never tell them what to do, because it's NOT going to happen. Let them do it themselves. You have no choice.

INFLUENCE or 'I'

Influence or 'I' pertains to oriented people who are highly sociable, excellent communicators, warm, trusting and "just want to have fun." They're 15% of the population. They are the type of people that make great sales. They jump from one program to another, looking for fun. These are very creative people with magnetic personalities. They want to look at the big picture and don't want to be bothered with the details.

How to Sponsor an 'I'

With an 'I' person, talk excitedly, be excited. Talk about partying, going golfing; sky diving, scuba diving, cricket and a lot of fun activities. They love having fun, fun and more fun. That's what they love and want to talk about all the time. "Hey, when you meet me at the dance, I'll be wearing a Hawaiian shirt. You'll recognize me. I'll have a big, funny hat on." They love to talk about how they will be spending the holidays with their family. They will join your team if you can get them excited and show how it will be fun to do so.

SUBMISSION or 'S'

'S' are patient and persistent people and form about 35% of the population. They're the analytical type of people. They analyze everything to death. They miss millions of dollars of opportunities because they keep analyzing. They usually delay their actions. They want to proceed at a steady pace and don't like sudden change.

How to Sponsor a 'S'

'S' believe that they're the smartest people on the planet. Within 2-3 minutes of talking, you'll know you have an 'S' type. They want all the details of the business.

You can never sell them anything, don't even try because you will fail. They have to sell it to themselves first. They'll listen to the conference call. Then they'll go to the website and check every link. If you have 25 links on your website, they'll check them all. <u>They will Google, go to YouTube, they'll read all the testimonials and the articles. Don't try and go too fast. Give them all the information. Be upfront.</u> Answer all their questions. Give them more websites to visit for information.

If you call them to answer questions, they will get upset. They will perceive you as being too pushy. Let them analyze the information at THEIR pace. In a week or two, they'll call back for more information or be ready to start. This is when they have already sold the idea to themselves and decided that this is the perfect business for them. <u>If you are patient, you will win them over.</u>

COMPLIANCE or 'C'

'C' adheres to rules, regulations and structures. They make up 35% of the population. They are nurses, schoolteachers and scientists. They work from the heart. They have time for everybody but not for themselves. The 'Cs' have built some of the largest organizations in network marketing ...That is WHEN they have the belief that they can do it.

How to Sponsor a 'C'

'Cs' don't want to be sold. They don't like pushy, aggressive salespeople. <u>Slow down the pace when you talk with a 'C'. Contain your excitement</u>. Lower the volume. They see the excitement as hype, and that you trying to sell them something. Don't tell a 'C' about making $20,000 a month, because it will turn them off. Instead, <u>talk less about business. Steer the discussion towards their family, children, and their holidays</u>. They love a compensation plan where you can put people under people and work in depth. They are best in any type of "infinity" plan that pays them to work deep. They love "Spillovers" in matrix plans.

TO SPONSOR YOU HAVE TO BE LIKE A CHAMELEON. YOU HAVE TO UNDERSTAND AND CHANGE COLOURS TO SUIT THE PERSONALITY TYPE

SMART WAY# 4: MENTORING/ TRAINING THE RIGHT WAY

I would like to emphasize again that network marketing is not a direct sales business. It is a mentoring and teaching business. To succeed, you have to learn to mentor and teach others. The first step to mentoring and training is to be teachable yourself. *Your income will be directly related to how fast you learn the business and be able to teach it to others who joined your team.*

To succeed in this business, you have to keep things simple. It is the KISS principle that you have to follow.........KEEP IT SIMPLE STUPID. You will need to teach a proven and tested duplication system that ordinary folks can understand. <u>The system you teach has to be very simple or it will not be duplicated by ordinary members of your team.</u>

Everyone you sponsor and their own sponsors need a step-by-step system to get their business to a fast start. The system must also help to develop the individual member's personality and build leadership. A person does not need all the techniques to be successful, but the system should make few available options so that a person can choose what is best suited to his personality. The system should be graduated to teach new skills as a person's business grows. There is no point in creating an information overload.

The initial training must include product training, business plan and information regarding the company and the industry. The new person must be advised to go on auto-ship and start using the products. This increases the belief system of an individual. There are people who try and build business by not using the product to save costs. This is a penny-wise foolish approach that should be discouraged at all costs.

The initial training should be followed by demonstration of how to conduct a home meeting. A successful home meeting is the essence of network marketing. <u>Attending big seminars and rubbing shoulders with the successful marketers can do wonders for the belief system but is not a system that can be duplicated by ordinary folks. They might shy away from the business thinking that it is not possible for them to speak with confidence to larger audiences</u>.

Whatever you practice and teach, it must be simple enough for ordinary people to duplicate. Otherwise, you will never be able to leverage your time and effort.

SMART WAY# 5: GET INTO PROFIT THROUGH BREAK- EVEN ANALYSIS

The purpose of starting a business is to make a profit. If a business spends more money than it makes, then it will belly up. So why should network marketing be any different?

We know that network marketing gives exponential passive income with time. If you have a group of 100 to 1,000 people in your network who are buying the products and recruiting more, then you will be getting richer and richer! *We all know that.*

It's SURVIVING the first 3 to 6 months in the business that is crucial. There is a learning curve involved ....typically a new distributor will go through three months of trial and error period. There is a learning curve involved ....typically a new distributor will go through three months of trial and error period. After which it takes 3 to 6 months to build a network that starts paying you money. If you can learn to manage your cash flow wisely, and also teach the people you sponsor to do the same , then you will succeed in this business.

The key to survival is CASH FLOW. People in network marketing usually run out of cash flow normally after 3 months, and they quit because they have not planned properly. If you teach and help the new members in your team to reach break-even as fast as possible ....It will give them confidence to continue in the business.

TYPICAL EXPENSES

A typical network marketing business will have the following expenses:

<> Joining Fee

<> Auto-ship

<> Petrol

<> Training Material

<> Promotion materials

<> Meetings and Rallies

<> Phone Bill

<> Leads

<> Advertising

<> Miscellaneous

People, when joining the business only look at the initial costs of joining and auto-ship. They fail to take into account other expenses that are vital to succeed in business. This results in cash crunch and dropping out of business.

BUDGETING AND REDUCING COSTS

To succeed, you have to budget your expenses and find ways and means to reduce costs. There are unscrupulous people in this business who make new members spend on advertising and promotional materials from which they generate revenues to run their own business. Advertising and promotion is essential to the success of any business but has to be done sensibly. Every dollar spent must show some positive results for the business, or it is a waste.

Spending money on your education first is the best investment you will ever do. If you are educated, then you will save thousands of dollars in the course of your business. There is simply no substitute for education. Find a mentor with a servant's heart who will coach you for free. Even if you have to pay a little money, do not hesitate. You will get exponential results from this investment. You have to invest in your education first, because as discussed earlier in this book-- network marketing is a mentoring business and not a sales business. You have to learn before you can teach.

Some other suggestions to reduce your costs are given below:

<> Keep minimum stocks necessary to run your business. Some stocks are necessary to share the experience with other people, but keep it to the minimum. You can always order more when you need them. If you have too much stock in your garage, then sell it to generate cash flow. It will give a new lease of life to your business.

<> Have a buddy in your area. This will not just save costs when traveling to meetings but will also create synergy.

<> Do some research and switch to low cost-phone plans. There are many free systems like SKYPE available on the internet.

<> To save petrol costs, try and qualify your leads before you decide to drive down and meet them. If you are prospecting someone who is indecisive, lazy and complains constantly, it is better to keep him or her in the back burner and focus on people who are excited about the business. You don't want to find yourself driving miles just to talk to someone and after two hours find out that they are not interested. A very good way to qualify what type of prospect you are dealing with is to ask few questions about their dreams and self-development. If you find that they have no energy in their words, or are not doing anything to improve themselves, then you can very well save lots of time and petrol.

<> As your network grows, you will have to find leaders in your team who are highly motivated and work with them for the betterment of the team.

<> The most important cost in your business is the leads and how you generate them. The cost of generating the leads and converting them into your business can be so huge that I will devote a separate section to this topic. You have to learn how to

minimize these costs and be effective. This is something you should understand and perfect it if you have to succeed in this business.

<> Hold local training sessions *(besides that of the company)* with all your team members. This may save costs to your team members.

<> Educate all the team members about proper cash flow management when building the business.

<> **Everyone must focus on following the same system in your team!** It is crucial for duplication. Can you imagine 100 people all going in their own direction? This is a recipe for disaster. A simple system of duplication saves costs, time and effort of the team.

TAX DOLLARS CAN FUND YOUR BUSINESS

Most governments give huge tax incentives to people engaged in home business. This is because it is good for the economy. Employment is a political issue for governments. They encourage people to start small businesses that hopefully will grow into big corporations someday. This is why governments give huge tax breaks if you start your own home business. If you are a paid employee on a fixed income, it is always smart to start a part-time home business to take advantage of the tax incentives provided by the government.

What most people do not realize is that the biggest chunk of cash outflow from their pockets is taxes. These can range anywhere from 20% to 55% of the income. This is huge in terms of dollars. When you engage in network marketing business, you can claim cost of communications, travel, entertainment, advertising and office stationary. You can even claim for products that you bought through auto-ship used for promotion as legitimate business expense.

You can claim part of your electricity, water bills, rates, house insurance and rent/mortgage as legitimate expenses for running a home office. You can also claim depreciation on your computer, office furniture, car, fax machine and other items that you need for your home business.

You can claim back the GST on items you purchased to run your business. You will need to register for GST before making any claims. As tax laws are different in each country, you will need to talk with your local tax consultant.

What these tax breaks do is give you huge cash flow to run your business. You can claim back the taxes paid and get a refund to run your business. In case there are unrecovered losses, then these can be carried forward and claim it back when your business starts to generate income the following year.

The tax incentives, in most cases, are so generous that they can fund your network marketing business in the initial stages. The break-even point of your business is much closer than you think when you take tax incentives into account.

Please do not join network marketing just to get tax refunds. You have to be active in the business to claim refunds; otherwise the taxman will come knocking on your doors. Having said that, tax incentives provide a huge motivation to start your home-based business and save on those dollars that will invariably go to the taxman-- never to be seen again.

Network marketing is without doubt the best route to start your own home business and get on to the road to financial freedom. It is the best program if you are looking for an early retirement.

Make sure your team members succeed. When you help them make money, they will help YOU make money!

SMART WAY# 6: MAKE USE OF TECHNOLOGY TO GROW YOUR BUSINESS

The greatest leverage you have to grow your business rapidly and with minimum effort is to make use of technology. Internet is changing the way people think and do business. It is also changing the way people communicate and build relationships. You can exchange ideas and interact with hundreds of like-minded people around the globe without ever having to meet them in the physical world. As a result, numerous social and dating websites have sprung up all over the internet and are gaining popularity.

Network marketing and the internet are made for each other. If you are not using the internet to build your network marketing business, then you are only running on one leg. Through the medium of internet, you can reach people across the globe who are interested in starting their home-based business because of the advantages it offers.

You can now have a home business that has a global reach. The biggest problem is that most ordinary folks do not understand this technology and how to reach the target audience to share their opportunity. There are thousands of websites that are being created each day and tons of information that gets loaded in the World Wide Web. It is not only enormous but exponentially grows every minute. The challenge is to reach the target audience with a minimum amount of fuss and expense.

The problem is compounded with the so called 'Gurus' who have all the fancy gadgets of ad blasters, blog blasters, banners etc. The idea is to throw in as much as you can into the already-over-expanding information web with the hope that someone will by accidentally click on your website and look at your opportunity. The probabilities of this happening are one in a trillion. It is a total waste of your time, effort and money.

Most of these so-called internet gurus are dishonest people who teach you outdated methods and their only interest is to sell you gadgets that are outdated. Internet is changing so fast that what works today will not work tomorrow. The only aim of these gurus is to lighten your pockets by selling strategies and gadgets that no longer work.

Internet is by far a free and large medium. It is not necessary to spend large amounts of money. All you need is a little bit of education.

You can reach your target audience by creating a niche for yourself. You have to reach out to people who have a problem. You have to offer a tangible solution and build a relationship of trust. It needs integrity and hard work. Most people look at the internet as a means of making a fast buck with minimum effort. Their greed gets them to the direction of sharks who offer them promise of instantaneous wealth. There are some very simple free strategies. Please read on........

GIVE AWAY FREE PRODUCT, SERVICE OR INFORMATION AND START A VIRAL FEVER

One of the best ways to establish a new relationship is to give FREE something that will be of value to the client. Everyone loves presents. A free gift works better than any advertisement. It establishes a bond of faith between the giver and the receiver. A gift is from the heart. It speaks of abundance.

People come to the internet for information. They don't come to the internet to view advertisements. They come to look for quality information. People also hate to pay too much for the information. If you do not have products of your own to give away to serve your audience then you can use MyLeadSystemPro who give you not only valuable lead magnets but also readymade sales funnel with email follow ups to build relationship with your leads on autopilot.

I am providing quality information regarding network marketing based on my experience at a very low cost to anyone who wishes to start his or her own home business. I am giving new faith to those who have tried and given up on network marketing. The information I am providing will work for any network marketing company. It is a gift from me to the industry for having given me so much more apart from the financial freedom.

I have met new people and made wonderful friends. It is a gift to the people whom I have not yet met but would like to meet and share my enthusiasm. They are in no way obliged to join my business. It is part of my vision to help people create long term wealth because poverty is the biggest curse on this planet. My mission in life is to help people generate sustainable residual income through proper education.

SMART WAY# 7: THERE IS FORTUNE IN FOLLOW-UP

The final technique I want to share with you is following up. If you have ever heard the term *"The fortune is in the follow up..."* you would be wise to take this to heart as a gospel truth. If you aren't following up, you are not building a relationship.

Network marketing, as I have explained earlier is all about building relationships, mentoring and teaching. If you do not have strong follow-up system in place, your business will not grow and sustain itself. *Follow-up takes time, effort and energy.* Most people fail because they do not have a system in place for sustained follow-up.

Chapter 4

The Final Secret

Let me now tell you my final secret that has increased income from my network marketing business tenfold.

According to my experience, the traditional way of network marketing business is dead. Selling overpriced juices and health products by conducting home meetings and dragging people to network marketing seminars is simply too tedious and time consuming.

Why should anyone join a network marketing effort that is so difficult? I have a close friend who is a Triple Diamond in his network marketing company. I shudder at the routine he follows. His meeting diary is filled from morning until night. He is earning passive income of around $600,000 per year. This excites me into joining a network marketing business. However, when I look deeply into his lifestyle I am a bit puzzled. After having worked so hard for the past 25 years with the company and building his network, he should be having free time to spend with his family. He is financially secure but where is the lifestyle?

I analyzed my friend's problem. The problem is in the retention rate. In traditional internet marketing business, the retention rate is only around 8%. If you are extremely skillful and have very good training systems (which my friend has got) then your retention rate can go up to 15%. If 90% of your affiliates are dropping out every year then you have to keep recruiting all the time.

My friend's company does not allow affiliates to have their marketing websites or advertise on the internet for the fear of misrepresentation of their products. They have a website with a back office to run the business, but affiliates are not allowed in marketing websites or blogs. This company is being overtaken by new generation of companies that are internet savvy and understand the power of this new medium.

Digital Product Companies

These days, I only promote network marketing companies that have digital products that can be delivered electronically. These can be educational products, marketing software and systems, wealth generation systems, entertainment and gaming products.

Why should you choose to promote these companies? First, the present generation wants instant gratification. Electronic products can be delivered instantaneously. There is no waiting time. Second, the cost of production of these products is minimal. There is the initial development cost. After which, there is no production or delivery cost. As a result, the profit margins are extraordinarily high.

Traditional MLM companies share 20 to 30 percentage profits. Most digital companies pay in excess of 50% of the profit share. The retention rate of these companies is over 90%. Why should anyone leave the company if they break even with just two or three sales?

Worldwide Reach

Most digital products can be sold worldwide without any limiting restrictions by local governments. Company marketing health products will need to get approval from the local authorities. They will need to register and set up distribution centers. Some governments insist on setting up local manufacturing facilities. This delays the launch and expansion of a company in new markets.

The physical products, if they are high-tech, also need to be demonstrated as they may have safety and health issues. This may require your physical presence in a new country of launch until such time you can train some local leaders in your organization. It all adds up to your time, effort and marketing costs.

Digital products have no such restrictions. They do not require any government approvals. Most network marketing companies launch digital products on a worldwide basis. Imagine the earning and potential power you get when you join any of these companies.

Life Style Business

Most digital MLM companies, because of their innovations, understand the internet marketing needs of their affiliates. They design business systems to help their affiliates market their business on the internet. This reduces time and effort to build a business.

Internet also provides technological leverage in which most marketing tasks can be automated. Alternately, you can outsource these tasks to India or Philippines where the labor is cheap. Once you automate your business you can relax on the beach, and the money will flow into your bank account night and day, 7 days a week.

A digital network marketing business once set up correctly, requires virtually no time or effort from you. You will need to devote time in setting up your systems and in improving them as technological advancements take place.

Digital MLM businesses give you lifestyle. These days, I sell my lifestyle as a marketing tool. Why should someone in his right mind get engaged in a traditional network marketing business when it is so simple and profitable to run a digital MLM business?

It must, however, be noted that your digital network marketing will need all the ingredients like relationship building, training, belief system etc. that I have discussed in the earlier part of the book for a traditional network marketing business. The principles do not change. Only the methodology of doing business changes on the internet.

Multiple Streams of Income from residual income

I am a strong believer in creating multiple streams of residual income. I have written a best-selling book on the subject titled **'How to Grow Rich by Creating Multiple Streams of Income'**.

In today's world, product life cycles have reduced to the extent that companies go out of business within a very short span of time. There is hardly any job security. The skills that you possess may become redundant or be shipped to another country where the labor is cheaper. In such environment, it is very crucial for you to have multiple sources of residual income and not rely on any one source of income.

Digital network marketing companies, because they take so little of your time, make it possible to engage in more than one business opportunity over the internet. The trick is to establish one network marketing business correctly, and then shift part of your profits to start another business.

To be successful, stick to the network marketing model selling- digital products on the internet. This is a proven formula for creating residual income that will help you to retire from your regular job within a remarkably short period of time.

If you liked the book and gained some knowledge that will be useful to you in life, then please leave an honest review to help others find this book. It will be a small effort on your part, but an act of charity that may help in changing few lives for the better. I thank you in advance for your help.

About the Author

Colin was abandoned by his father at the age of fourteen and joined the Navy at tender age of fifteen where education, roof and free rations were guaranteed.

To understand the root cause of suffering he turned towards philosophy and religion. One fine day he understood that 'life is 'and material and spiritual world are closely interwoven. You cannot live in one without the other.

One of the reasons he identified as root cause of his suffering was his deep seated financial insecurity resulting from his childhood deprivation. He took pre-mature retirement from the Navy after having successfully commanded submarines and set about building his financial future.

Colin strongly feels that it is only through increasing ones spiritual, emotional and financial intelligence can someone transform not only one's own life but also of his loved ones. He now writes books and articles on financial and spiritual matters to empower people to improve their lives.

Having seen poverty and depravation first hand, Colin's aim in life is to help people create wealth in an enlightened way. On his website http://wealth-creation-academy.com/ he teaches people how to Create Multiple Streams of Passive Income based on his personal experiences and experiments from being an abandoned child in a small town in a third world country with no prospects to owning several streams of income that has made him wealthy.

www.ingramcontent.com/pod-product-compliance
Lightning Source LLC
Chambersburg PA
CBHW020845210326
41598CB00019B/1976